Death's Rehearsals

Sidra Sahar Imran

Translated by

Muhammad Azram

inner child press, ltd.

Credits

Author

Sidra Sahar Imran

Translator

Muhammad Azram

Editor

hülya n. yılmaz, Ph.D.

Cover Design

Saeed Ibrahim

General Information
Death's Rehearsals
Sidra Sahar Imran

1st Edition: 2021

Publisher Information:
Inner Child Press International
www.innerchildpress.com

ISBN-13: 978-1-952081-39-2 (inner child press, ltd.)

$ 10.95

Dedication

My Parents
Muhammad Imran and Zainab

My Mother In-Law
Nasim Akhter

My Husband
Muhammad Wasim Chaudhary

Table of Contents

The Poetry

Table of Contents . . . continued

Table of Contents . . . continued

Epilogue

Introduction

Art is a divine prism that reflects the true colors of life. Poetry has been one of the most beautiful colors as it continues reflecting on the horizon of life and imaginations. The rainbow of poetry is spread on the eternal canvas of life; not only blooming in the true colors of life but also as an authentic and divine color that highlights the grey and murky patches of life. William Wordsworth said, "Poetry is the spontaneous overflow of strong feelings" but it doesn't always take "its origin from emotion recollected in tranquility." Sometimes it takes its origin from grievous distress. In the words of Abdul Kalam, "poetry comes from the highest happiness or the deepest sorrow", and those of Lenard Cohen, "poetry is just the evidence of life. If your life is burning well, poetry is just the ash." While reading Sidra Sahar Imran, we come across such a situation that we cannot choose what a great poetry is: the one that takes its origin from tranquility, or the one that takes its origin from deepest distress.

Reading Sidra Sahar Imran was one such great experiences of surprise and awe. In Sidra's work, metamorphism and symbolism are flourishing at their best. With her unique words, terminologies and phrases, she demonstrates the gray and murky images of life using metamorphism. She uses unique and strong metaphors to reflect the life that is being lived around her. Metaphors like 'red color', to describe the blood of innocent people flowing in street; 'white color', to describe the coffins of people who are being killed in wars and explosions; 'black color', to describe unnatural death – which is being forced on innocent people, and 'barking dogs', to designate people whose uncontrolled and uncensored words are responsible for all the misfortunes of the world and its poor and helpless people. When I read her work for the first time three years ago, I not only was astonished but also witnessed the unique and diverse colors of life with infinite shades of gray. I have discovered novel and innovate expressions and definitions of happiness, sadness, pain and life.

This book has been originally written in Urdu through which Sidra penned down unfortunate stories of life from the streets and cities around her. She presents an account of the pain of life in her unique writing style with her grieving words and lamenting phrases to expose the real face of the world – a world that is full of injustice, pain, miseries, misfortunes, power and control, ammunition, explosions, rapes, and deaths. Her poems are metaphorically overflowing with the blood of innocent people, tears of unfortunate mothers, and unnatural deaths in streets. She laments the way how the life is being handled around her in particular, and throughout the world in general.

When I first read her astonishing verses, phrased in extraordinary words, exceptional and stinging terminologies, and unique phrases in her free-flowing thoughts, I wished to offer her literary talent to English-speaking readers. In my translation of her poetry, I have tried my best to preserve the spirit, flow and rhythm of the original work alive.

Muhammad Azram
Poet, Writer, Translator

Preface

The book in your hands, *Death's Rehearsals* (*Moot Ki Rehearsal* in Urdu) is my second book of poetry. I have written both in Urdu. My first book was titled *We: The Metaphors of Sin* (*Hum Gunah ka Istahara Hein* in its original language). I have stepped into the charismatic literary world in strange circumstances. From my childhood on, I fell in love with reading, and that love for books paved way to my writing endeavors.

I was brought up in a traditional and culture-focused family system in Pakistan. Reading literature was considered as a blatant thing for girls who are barred from reading any literature apart from religious texts. My parents were also very strict when family customs and traditions are concerned. At an early age, however, I have gathered some books and started reading. I never came face to face with my father because all my siblings and I were afraid to encounter his strictness. My mother found my books and burnt them all. According to her, books would make me shameless, bold and blunt, which was considered to be bad for girls. That event of "Thirty-three match sticks" turned my life around. A blunt and rebellious voice erupted from the ashes of my burnt books. Though that painful event made half-dead inside, it also jolted the sleeping writer inside me. I started writing fiction and literary texts, and started sending them to different journals and magazines with different pen names. Soon, I realized that sending with different pen names was a bad idea and not helpful at all. So, I started submitting my work with my real name. Though it was a risky approach with regard to me having to face my parents and family, in a short time, my name began to appear everywhere. The positive response and respect I had gathered from the people and critics were more than enough for my parents and family to realize that writing is a very respectable profession. They accepted my passion for writing. In my marriage, the All-Mighty blessed me with a very supportive husband who always stands by me.

After my heart-breaking experience of "Thirty-three match sticks", I started writing down everything for catharsis: broken pieces of poetry, fiction, novels and plays. I began to fade into writing the same things, stories, subjects and poetry. I realized that romantic poetry, fiction crafted on false and fake ideas and lengthy novels without any base and gain were not my business. I believed that I was born for something greater for a noble cause. Poetry always attracted me, and my inner rebellion began to pour out through poetry. Poetry allowed me to say what I wanted to say. When I started writing poems, there was plenty around me to write about. Fundamental rights violations, social injustice, discrimination, gender inequality, honor-killings, harassments, child abuse, religious and liberal extremism, explosions, and blood flowing like water in our streets.

When I kept witnessing the grievous reality of my society in particular and that of the world as a whole, I realized that the earthly sorrows are far greater than my own sorrows, and that they are far more horrible and atrocious. So, I started writing the pain of the Earth, became a voice for helpless people, and started penning poems in a highly unconventional way with a novel style and unique approach. Everywhere in the world, there is injustice, oppression, riots, division, lies, slander, oppression, violence, deceit, indifference, abductions, border disputes and death. To me, life seems to be an utterly grievous phenomenon, and a few self-centered people who are ruling this world are busy making it more unlivable. Though I live in an unsupportive society, I became one of most powerful voices against wars, injustice, fear, harassment, and social and gender inequality.

Though mine was a difficult journey, I didn't give up my passion to keep myself alive in murky environments. I was like a wave, like a rebellious symbol and an authentic reflection, showing this world the true colors of egoistical people and the harm which they have been inflicting on life and on our Earth.

My poems are voices for the vulnerable segments of society, melodies of those who cannot play their own music with free will, and a mosaic image of the world which no wants see or feel. Hopefully, my little effort will make people think and change the approach to life and living. I am grateful to Muhammad Azram for translating my poems into English so my literary voice can reach across the globe.

Sidra Sahar Imran

The Poetry

Death's Rehearsals

Sidra Sahar Imran

A Grave Takes Snaps

I traded the soil
But earth couldn't provide me a home
In making shelters
I engraved numerous patches in the sky
My lips got granular like my shoes
My hands pull me like wheels
I drive myself to you

God dragged out eyes
And . . . by making a heart from the soil
I remembered you
By dreaming
When yellow flowers
Start falling from air bags
I have listened last Adhan
You hired a hearse for me
And put my coffin in

What Happened to Our Nests?

The zesty scent of tears is in the air
The eyes of birds are looking
For light rays in those lime lines
Which are budding new trees
With the laces of old shoes
Our breaths are yellow leaves
We gifted our yellow dreams
To those seasons
Which didn't have their own feet
We walk on walls with our eyes
No window takes our hands
The story asks
Of which street our dreams turned lifeless

Sidra Sahar Imran

Can Water Pardon a River for Murder?

Our wellbeing
Fell on the rail tracks
Suspiciously
Winds before hiding the path from us
Haven't returned trees to birds
The address of our home
Imparted to stones
By that wall
In which love was inscribed
False and fabricated news
Are being blown out on streets
And . . .
On mobile screens
Our dissipated names
Jumped many nights
The sun within its civic
Broadcasting news of our enforced disappearance
Light is departed from our fortune lines
Let us send letters to darkness
Or else . . .
Kindles won't come to our graves
To protest!

We've Given Birth to Voices

We've beaten drums
On sleeping roads,
Washed dust with our eyes,
We bequeathed voices to walls,
And dumped the deafness of the city
We bestowed rainbow colors
To spat-on posters,
We've unchained those feet
Which swallowed our properties
With sliced pieces of rain from heaven
We cooled down the cellar of fire
We amalgamated hearts of broken widows
To make those doors
Which don't match with musty houses
And . . . after throwing outrageous voices on roads
We've revived those accents
Which were poisoned by waned thumbs

Breathing Is Forbidden

Two minutes of silence
For that added love
Whose height was not as much as the walls
And fears from seeing the sky
In the pink sack of it
In which butterflies of dead dreams
Carrying the camphor-scent
Snapped photos
In white outfits

On those days
When our time became too expensive
We fed ourselves with low-cost homilies
You used to drive on your feet
To bring flowers
On the way, starving kids used to
Offer us the sandwich of forged prayers
Alas! How could our lives
Amend calendars of their tents?

There is no color of ugliness
It can't fit to any illustration
Yes . . . love is obnoxious!

People
Can't tolerate it
Even for 2 minutes in a day

Unfaithful Life

Not bread
But we've stolen fire,
Not water,
But we've boiled stones,
Not shoes,
But we've worn roads,
Not birds,
But we've captured eyes,
Not ornaments,
But we've collected chains,
Not flowers,
but we've hauled thorns,
In prayers for rains
We've mortgaged our palms,
In the shapes of homes
We've renovated our graves,
We seeded our tears in heavens
To cultivate rains,
And throughout our lives
We've begged salt from life

Sidra Sahar Imran

We Are Standing on the Rooftop of Death

Some *Sajdah was peeping
Through the window of someone's forehead
We were completely messed up
We blindfolded our eyes
With the laces of patience
The pockets of our enemies
Were packed with angels
People like coffins
Want to give us a last bath
From the buckets of patience
They even don't know
That the life to the scope of disbeliefs
Turned adulterated!

*Sajdah is an Arabic word, meaning prostration to God in the direction of the Kaaba at Macca which is usually done during the daily Muslim prayers. The position involves having the forehead, nose, both hands, knees, and all the toes touching the ground together.

A Festival of Dead Flowers

That was the moment of love
When I took a float of flowers
From your hands
And grouped it in my hand
And . . . placing your parting evening
In my eyes, filled with salt,
Requested from the wind
To memorize my address
There was no grief for the wind
It was a talk about my death

Humiliating a Poem

It is quite possible
That some of my poems
Get sick from your sticky gestures,
It is quite possible
That some of my poems
Alter their way
After viewing your shadows,
It is quite possible
My loneliness tells lies to God
About you,
And . . . it is quite possible
God is used to laugh at me for a long time!

I Desire to Print Flowers on Your Lips

I discern a lesson of laughing
Without even learning it
And, on my turn to weep
My eyes turned impassive
He made tears from the soil,
From tears he prepared me for
And . . . of me, he organized death

You've sewn your pain
In my nights
And . . . after tearing my shirt
You made a boat for yourself
You can smoothly flow into me
But . . . I've admitted a strike of tears
Now the river barks at me

How infertile these mountains are
That one asks from that smile
Whose generation is demolished!

Sidra Sahar Imran

Earth, Full of Spittle

Have you ever met life?
Have you ever clapped with humor
After having an eye-to-eye interaction with it?
Have you ever called a dump tears
To come to you thru wrong signals?
Have you ever revolved
Around the heels of a heart
With your cheap eyes
And sprinkled flowers of dust?
Have you ever celebrated the festival of you?
Have you ever licked your saliva after spitting?
Have you even danced in stony valleys
After tying your eyes on your feet?
Have you ever dug wells on the name of your blood?
Deep within those wells, our dreams of shoes
Flow like buckets of water!
We have witnessed life
Netting net with useless papers.
We have witnessed smelling moments
Dumped in scum-filled smiles
Meeting with life.
Have you ever met life?
It is as ugly
As this earth is;
There is no tent on it that can fit in our shoes.

Fire and Blood
Are Our National Festivals

We revolve around
The heels of life,
We tie our eyes
In red hankies,
We want to touch heaven
Jumping on our scattered coffins
But our feet
Are sticky with blood

Our children
Like cheap toys
Are displaying on foot-paths
In the eons of water and ice
They play games of fire and blood
Our butterflies
Are slayed in jungles
Our fireflies
Turned into prison cells

Bullets like flies
Buzz around our heads
While signing our own death certificates
With our broken fingers
We are getting buried
In favorably furnished files of UNO

Sidra Sahar Imran

How Long Will Life Continue to Spit on Us?

We are the people
Rolling down from the plates of life,
Earth is spitting on us
From all, everywhere,
And . . . walls, by kicking
Throwing us out from them
The dwellers of the cities
Get showers of heavenly food
On us . . . afflict of double torment
Even then, we do not collect
Pieces of breads
From the messy drains of fortunes

Even today,
We haven't been able to behold true images
Of bread, clothes and shelters
We are like needles
Pierced in pale bricks of body
And from the dweller of *Kaaba
We purchase upturned bowls of mud
Dip ourselves deep within them
Till our bodies bruise till the nails
We . . . are more vicious than poison

Death plays **seven stones with us
In the vessels of fire
We Commence Olympics
By burning our eyes
Barefoot, we run fast . . . very fast
We . . . those, who can support
In the competitions of life;
Heaven rejects us from all directions

Simulated People like marble
Negate us like the sludge
(Some sprinkles do fall at the feet of God)

*Kaaba is a building at the center of Islam's most important mosque, Al Masjid Al Haram (The Sacred Mosque), in the city of Mecca, Saudi Arabia. It is the most sacred site for Muslims.
**"Seven stones" is a traditional Indian game.

Sidra Sahar Imran

Perfume

In the cracked
Shoes of water
A path is tacked
On a platter of lamps
I firmly place eyelids
Then a parting fragrance
Starts dispersing
From the ponds of black water
(A fragrance, similar to camphor)

Poems Written on Tents

I

Mother! I don't remember you
But on the walls of my childhood
An amply beaming woman is painted
Mother . . . you don't resemble that woman
How deep rains have drowned your eyes
I want to touch them with my lips
But my lips start undulating

II

Why doesn't heaven smile?
Have you traded?
The peace of a slumbering
Sleep
By trading hunger
Have you traded your happiness too?

III

Death has emptied both of my pockets
For me, my father was an ATM machine
The day I lost him
I haven't bought any happiness
My mother and my school bag
Both used to disperse the same fragrance
Both were blown up by a bomb explosion

Sidra Sahar Imran

IV

Four breads in four years
In the season of doves
If wheat is cultivated instead of bullets
Even then my hands
Become short of four breads
Alas! When will this little grave grow bigger?

This Time, God Will Spit on You

If you don't get full marks
In the mathematics of your corporeal appearance
Then I'll balance you with naked calls
Of your father and brother
After ripping off your eyes
I make those graves
Where you left the colors of butterflies
Scrolling like scorpions
In your illegitimate room
You're waiting for our heels
But we don't want to trade them
Against a mere few steps
We have knotted you up within the walls of murder
As long as your bones turn to that ash
Which our *Asifas sprinkle with their feet
When they go to meet God

*Asifa was the girl who was murdered in Kashmir after a gang rape. Here, this name was used in the plural form to represent all girls who were killed in the same way.

A Day Reserved for Poetry

How good I could be
If in 365 days of a year
To all rhymes
From those I smell frozen filth
Of dumped wells
It would be much better
To threw them in dirty drains
After filling them in plastic bottles

It would be much better
If infected poems with fungus
Trolled on roads
After filling them in iron drums
And they would've slipped away after rolling

It would be much better
From the sliced tongues of stolen words
To satisfy the hunger of sneaky poets
By getting gyrated to a staircase of stage
They come to your feet

It would be much better
From the forged documents of poetry
Those who lick the salt of fame
And name themselves as chains and rods
Or else, a dustbin
And pages decorated with expensive inks
Selling their substandard and cheap paintings
They turn into spat-out *Paan

*Paan is a combination of betel leaf with areca nut, widely
consumed throughout South Asia. It is chewed for psychoactive
effects. After chewing, it is either spat out or swallowed.

The Oath of Mumbling Dogs

I

You're a black nail
That is nailed in the earth-like sins
By tearing off the clothes of the soil
You made your turbans
And . . . murdered your motherland after gang-raping it
You're carrying flowers of slime in your hands
The sky considers you a spit-box
And trees consider you . . . a spit of disgrace
But
There are few faithful who are like that too
Those who don't wish to illegitimate these chins

II

If
The keys of your eminence
Got blind after falling in a main hole
And . . . those crows
Who laugh at pigeons
Continue to cultivate hunger strikes
On the chests of infertile lands
And their self-respect
Get sliced from your nails
And your shameless eyes play tambourine
Making them dance in the nude

III

Those who make tombs of their graves
For themselves
After licking your feet
If they are able to see their own feet
They would understand
What they consider as anklets
Spittle is filled in the linkages of those chains

Which Country Shall We Be Questioning?

We are not forbidden bites
That you throw at us after eating the half of them
How many generations
We've thrown into the furnace of your pride
Made how many mothers pregnant to guard your borders
How many headscarves were twisted into a hanging noose?
How many eyes were pulled out to wash
  the stains on flags?

When the shouts of bullets
Say Adhan in the ears of our children
We blast numerous balloons of ammunition
To celebrate festivals of the white color

We're the people who got stuck between borders
We got separated from our herds
Now these pigs, hunter dogs, jackals and wolves
Are being written into vacant spaces
As parents of our children

The City Is Peeled Off

The road that was murder
In the name of hatred
You attributed to us that road
We . . . as an announcement for disappearance
Are being displayed on walls

On those days
When we used to spend our days
By stitching slogans
And used to think that the soil can't provide us water
You provided us homes made with flags
And ordered us to give up our rights on oceans
Then we, after digging our eyes,
We used to discover a peeled-off city
And used to ask the roads
Why 'you' are being engraved on our roads

There Is No International Day for People Who Are Being Rejected by Life

That dance has perished
Which couldn't find any thread
To religion
Those steps have gone mad with the fear of death
Those that used to revolve on pulleys of an eye!
All those that got perished
Who used to ask the meaning of life!
And . . . that time was thrown into mourning wells
That used to tie ropes at the feet of death

Have you listened to the explosion?
Have you listened to the call of death?
Have you taken nude pictures of the Doomsday?
We are the fear of life!

An examination of those bodies
Whose eyes were engraved alive
We, after being rejected by ourselves
For which soil we should sing the song;
That asks questions about God
And . . .
After getting parted from God
We're being killed
After a humiliating joint grave

Sidra Sahar Imran

Why Is a Man a Sacred Place and a Woman Is a Lamp?

A woman slid away from that very eye
That was tied with her black shawl
And fingers were lost in a multitude of doors
On which lip, you've decorated the name "plaque" of you
On which hand, you dug your path
The stone asks . . .
My question is far from your limited reach
But earth knows
That, in the memory of every man,
Dwells many women
And . . . for every woman, there is only one man
I was a woman too
Before God was discovered

A Sale on Graveyards

When we just thought about the wall
People
Started bringing their placards
And . . .
Squeezing cries from sold slogans
We got busy in forming joints of chains
We saw feet resembling bricks
And thought,
How our last house will look like
When the identity from doors is taken away
People . . .
We shall ask God by showing hands
Who will die first

Puzzles That Were Solved

With a price tag
Of eighty or hundred lashes
The dignity of a woman can be bought,
But a man doesn't sell his manhood
He smells childhood's clothes
On the prescriptions of an herbal medicine
And continues doing business by collecting dolls

When a slight moaning
Turns to streaks of blood
Then the focus of the camera
Revolves everywhere
And those who increase the yield
Of wheat crops
Don't agree
To let stocks out from their warehouses
At the corner of streets
Straying eyes guard them
Till the time when the armpits get green again

People Walking on Wheels

No city fits in those feet
The chapters of their homelessness
Are written on the last page of earth

Even a seven-yards-long tongue
Of a sky cannot reach the sunshine
Of those lethal feet

The charity committee of ants
Left shattered sacks of flour
On the banks of rivers
Where prostitute fishes
Give birth to those feet
From their wombs
Those which do not fit in any city!

Sidra Sahar Imran

International Day of Coffins

On the ugly walls of death
They were tossed
Like spit
And are being written
Like vulgar slogans
And . . . after vacating a flower-like city
They were distributed freely
Dead in a graveyard

O Love, Curses on You!

I

No one measures anyone's grave
No one picks the white colors
From someone's colors
No one creates oceans
After flowing from someone's eye
No one clears someone's path
All is theatre, all is bullshit
Look . . . I'm alive
Look . . . you're alive
I'm dawning on someone else's body
And you're playing in the mud
Of someone else's body
I'm feeling at home in the shelters of my grieves
And you're reaping someone else's pain
Look . . . you smile and cry with him
And you get mad in laughing
I am also licking someone else's wounds
Sharing someone's grief
I too laugh my heart out
And cry my heart out
You're the morning and evening of someone else
I'm also translating someone's day into night

II

Look . . . my inner self was filled with you
But . . . now, the many mirrors of your name
Break inside me occasionally
Even then, I don't remember you
I spit on your memories
You may get shocked listening to my name
Then abuse this love by calling names of mother and sister

(That swallowed many years of you)
Look . . . I became venomous
Look . . . distance doesn't hurt me
I want to cross your way once
And want to pour my venom on your lips
That has stung my loneliness
I wish to be available to myself to that extent
That I could write a letter to God
Writing details of your misconducts
If God knows it all
I want to know all crimes of you from Him
Look . . . I want to sting you!

Why the Barrenness of Earth Doesn't Grow Trees

(In December, not snow but fire falls)
Now, gravestones on deep cold graves
Would be dried up with black sunshine
And . . . and time will be moving on its third foot
Last year
When half-yard long shadows
Made bubbles from red water
Then an eagle emerged from the eight line of the sky
And . . . the entire forest has gone bare

Those who went for hunting
Invented a forest
With scars of blood
Taken from school's walls
Demonstrated a holiday
People gathered walls
To display calendars
That are being fulfilled by vacations

We cherish our tears like expired breads
Made shoes of those tents
Which were filled with
Sulfur, coal, and potassium nitrate
Now, time wants to walk barefoot

Coffins Left as Inheritance

When trees get empty of light
We . . . post our poems in gray envelopes
Which we've written with the sunlight
For those eyes
Which gave birth to dead dreams

When the staircases of age
Get tired of numbering themselves
In the shades of those roofs
We've wrongly written in home's classification
We'll turn into a substandard house
And . . .
We shall be left
Against a baseless piece of earth
A mortuary
Placed in the fifth corner of the city

Paralyzed Dreams and Sticks of Eyes

People getting ink from walls
Can go against a bright day
Can tie the dancing ankle-bells
In the feet of the twilight
But can't cut the hands
Of those trees
Those which erased the story
Of the jungle after writing it

When the soil tends to dance
Things leave their places
And . . . we, by getting misguided by heaven
Start lamenting the earth
You, by pouring our shares of brick
Into your eyes
Can build such a home
Where our dreams can dwell
Till that night
That can't succumb before your eyes

Sidra Sahar Imran

Worshippers of Guns

From armpits of them, those gods appear
And women . . .
Throw them away like sins
On unmarked roads
They can't smell flowers of the Judgment Day
Within them, everyone carries a decreeing power
Where it is written with an axe
"Death Plenty"
Nothing less, nothing more
No image can be drawn from their faces
Their eyes
Resemble that crime
Which had been committed
By a woman on her wedding night

You Can't Get Off a Woman

Your eyes can handle
All the nudity of the world
And . . . your fortune lines on hands
Can be referred to vulgar signs on a terrace
Can you discuss it again with God
On concerns of your bodily configurations?
Alas!
In the meaning of good virtues
Men
Can be used excessively in those phrases
With those connotations
That turned you crooked
And . . . doubled the taste of your tongue

Sidra Sahar Imran

Star Number 2016

Before touching drums
Our hands are butchered off
Wolves . . .
On that night
When *Yousef brought a shirt
The well had been filled with red color
Slowly . . . slowly
Those jungles
Which were being abducted by cities
Stopped growing **Yaqoob's Eyes

*Prophet Joseph (May peace be upon him)
**Prophet Jacob (May peace be upon him)

The War Written Before Love Letters
(We take refuge from the fire and ammunition)

We don't want to be a part of a joint grave
To show the hatred for the color of red
We should demonstrate the excavation soil
People who dream upended on shoulders of uniforms
Ammunition walks on the streets of city
In place of people

Bells after lamenting temples
Now they're taking places of sirens in ambulances
And . . . the after the beginning
The season of slings
White color
Won't witness the measurements of any body
Doors will have to see with open mouths
To those hands . . .
Which haven't reached their necks yet

Sidra Sahar Imran

Thirst Thrown into Euphrates

A spring can bloom on dead branches
Till the bit of last breath
But that could be so painful
That . . . even an ocean starts thinking of suicide
People don't allow our rivers to slip off of their hands
We on Hussain's name
Have poured vouchers into those eyes
Due to their blindness
Our eyes are getting blind too
When thirst is being squeezed
From our bodily dwellings
Then a new Hell will welcome us
And . . . we,
In connection of preserving water unlawfully
Turned all the blessings of God
Forbidden for us

Love in Nirvana

When sunbeams used to blaze my feet
You fetched for the twilight in your eyes
And spread it unto the reach of my pathways
Do you remember?
How long on the roads
We elongated each other's rumination
Long before our departure
Birds composed many stories of us

Now when fading evenings grow in the sky
And I visualize those clouds
Those which condemned our afternoons
The blazing heat choked us for hours in her darkness
We blazed ourselves barefoot with trees
Without the consciousness
That our feet will get vanished by melting

Look, how our love turned us
Like poems engraved in June and July
And . . . after bearing a long night
The sun will not disappear anywhere
Escaped from my inner-self!

Sidra Sahar Imran

A Number Plate Posted on a Graveyard

When his hands were as solid as a gravestone
Like a grave, I was filled from the inside
From the day when he calligraphed my name
The sunlight hasn't come down from the mountains
I sailed away with rains
And breeze kept on calling me
But . . . my feet didn't know
That . . .
One way also opens to a back street
He hasn't reached to me
Jumping from the window of his house
He transfigured into a gravestone

The Third Episode of a Story

We're the last date of a bath board
Or . . . the First day of Thorne
The imperative of this illusion
Going to be decreed by that tree
That fetches us to sin
Into street number 3
When mistake was not invented
Hands didn't eat the bite to get together
We are the process of before and after the coffin
You're a never written mourn
And, I am . . . confiscated history

Sidra Sahar Imran

I Endorse the Point of View
of the Darkness

We celebrated the festival of abuse
And . . . made flags of tearing off collar
When the festival of our hatred is being celebrated
Then our languages turn to spit boxes
How much can you spit?

With these fingers,
The soil of how many graves
Have we gathered
Those which were being created for a symbol?

Which road invented you?
Which red light will teach you how to speak?
Who will sell his eyes, fearing you?
You will have to speak nonsense
The sun can't fight your case

We Are Far More Beautiful Than Death

We have experienced that quietness
By staying in the city of voices
That was more exquisite than life
When you couldn't derive any meanings of eyes
Apart from tears
Then rains stopped weeping

Have you heard the silence of the earth?
If not . . . then you envision me by parting from you
Who will identify you within me?
Who can tell
How many graves travel to each other?

Sidra Sahar Imran

Advertisement Is Forbidden

Virtuous lady
She can dance wearing a scarf,
She can tie ankle-bells . . . of numerous eyes,
And she can drink herself
After pouring herself into drinks

She can turn numerous thrones of corporeal
She can like for herself thousand-miles-stretched eyes
She can turn herself to a wall
In which . . . some . . . something . . . could be written!

Love Has Melted

We've lost the moons of our eyes
And begged from the nights
We burned those evenings into ashes
By the heat of the sun
This used to steal our way
After collaborating with the treacherous walls
    of your house
The insanity of dust
Swallowed our profound fear
We, like snakes, followed your life
And like poison, we poured you in our veins!

Sidra Sahar Imran

Relationship Is a Torn-Off Shirt

In his salary pack
He sent me a wrapped quest
How many images an eye can draw
That is being filled with ink

I made a dream
Equal to the grains of sand on my feet
And rolled that dream into water

When the ocean didn't listen
Then . . . I chanted against boats
And killed islands like Love

Bury me in my eyes
A white color can't replicate me

In Our Streets, Catastrophes Give Birth to Children

We are those bad names
Those who wear sunshine in their feet,
And . . . and with our eyes
We've witnessed the rape of the night
The night that was in a marriage contract with some day
Was killed by the hands of the sun

Our sins grow like trees
We . . . by sitting under their shades
Play with the toys named self-esteems and egos
One day, they will transform into brothels
With our smelling bodies
The dogs which luster the gravedigger's nights
Will bestow upon us their luxuries in succession

Bastards! For God's sake,
Pray for our infertility!

Sidra Sahar Imran

War for a Piece of Bread

In that festival
When God was asking for eyes
We said . . .
Don't ask for our sons
We kept our mother safe
And . . . donated our sons to mountains

When ammunition's day arrives
Coffins turn to numbers

Food distributors said, eat roads
And drink sweat
Light doesn't like you
You're religious to the last extent of ignorance
Why do your throats remain open like key holes?
How long will you keep begging?
The water distributors said
We've cracked begging bowls . . . you cut off your hands
(Bastard, you speak shit)

The Story Turned into a Gravestone

In empty inkpots
We gathered the ink of corruption's day
And wrote a few nights
Those cannot be smashed before the waning of poison

Assuming ourselves a fancy story
We went to the city
To narrate ourselves as a tale
But the tongue
Got stuck between jaws and didn't utter a single word
People started barking in sign languages
And . . . the graveyard woke up!

I Have to Hire a Lawyer for My Mother; Will You Share the Cost?

Have counted . . . full 365 days
But . . . unable to gather charity of a single moment for you
Mother! They have put you in the cold house
And the only way into it drives from some verse
   of the Quran

Mother!
There is no day left for you
But . . .
But when some nude mistake undresses itself
Then people say by securing their necks
That . . . Eve from the downlines of centuries
Is a metaphor for sin!

Mother!
Though my elegiac relationship is illiterate
Far from the noble book of goodness
But . . . do tell to her judge
That . . .
He should take back your sin from the dwellers of the earth

Mother!
Why you don't tell God
That you're not responsible
For the abandoning of my father from heaven?

Mother!
Those who are consuming your share
Landed in hell by tracing your footprints

Hands Full of Hell

Our eyes could handle fire
But
How many letters
God has written to the river
But they haven't reached our eyes

You presumed fire
As your self-esteem and ego
And burned girls
In place of woods
You thought religion as a bullet
And . . .
After sending all those words to our funerals
You've opened the outlets of ammunition

You assumed a funeral as a festival
And celebrated it in every city
Our mountains laugh seeing you
Overjoyed, laughing twists their intestines
Twists in intestines
And those twists
Remind us of your turbans
Prayers went unheard for those who died
Let us remember the unadorned calls

Sidra Sahar Imran

The Dowry

We heard

The news of our death

And wrote on a gravestone

We saw a dead body

And asked for a coffin

Meaning, 'you'!

Let Us Rehearse Death

When from the depth of trenches
Creams arise
We design ambulances on our palms
When crutches walk
On rough paths . . . stooping
Then clouds run for taking our hand
Mountains give us an angry look
As we've chained down their feet
Someone can block our hearing powers
It is necessary
That
By putting our bodies in corners
The song of Death would be sung
We could be deaf

Sidra Sahar Imran

Birds Trained on Poles

Trees dig their address
On the hands of unpaved roads
But the chain of wet soil
Doesn't match
The prints of their feet

When day registers on a charity register
Those laments
Readers of those laments
Leave on full afternoons
Then sunlight wails on the highways
And
Air starts dwelling in a nest

By the Time . . . Indeed, Humankind Is in a Loss

Someday, like the one . . . approaching
When God would say
That the bricks
Those that have been collected
In the name of God
Are not profitable to Him
Then collect hands
Those who lost the breaths of prayers

Sidra Sahar Imran

Memorial Tickets of Eyes

You will die
And from our bodies
A desert will emerge
Where, when the night falls,
In bowls of stars
Stones of light shall break,
And we'll be bought and bring in your eyes

You will die
The city will travel to a tale
Love with the support of an image
Will be renovated on the chest of a wall
Flowers . . . so many flowers
Will stand tall on soil
Placing foot alongside foot
Don't know . . . which prayer is getting late

You will die
The house will get old
And will bend after getting very old
To the feet of the earth
And on graves with a new red shine
A path will invert into a new page

You will die!

A History of the Jungle

At that time
When the axe was invented
After a needle
It forced those trees to eat insects
Those were not as unashamed
As men were
Those who lived in caves
Took all the leaves with them
And the bare trees
Got together in the jungle
For their fundamental rights

To fail a successful strike
The fire of the jungle was taken to the cities
And in the history of man
Communal killing started
For many days, woods were put on fire
Alongside with men

Wait . . .

The Sun

Turned dry

Standing in the garden

But . . . no one dragged the veil

Eyes got very cold

Like those hands

Which became lifeless resting on pillows

And . . . in bowls,

Wax keeps on filling

Man Placed in the City's Pocket

In the city of pickpockets
A blind man sells used dresses
To buy a pair of shoes

Rats throw his shoes
Into the sewage
And he eradicates his feet
With a sand paper

Man exchanges his MP3 player
With the voice of that woman
Whose voice is more tortured than drums
That woman could shout so loudly
If man can tell him
That his ears are frozen
With extreme coldness

Sidra Sahar Imran

Time Died of Starvation

If this earth

Gets upside down

Then from it

Those dresses will emerge

Which will take away

Half of our food

The Last Stage

Advice is written on a prescription

Morning, Afternoon, Evening;

2 tablets

For that love

Which have been tossed

Into someone's life

Rather than throwing it into a dustbin

Sidra Sahar Imran

Showers of Doves

Can this earth
Sign a marriage contract with us?
Why this sky-like roofs of iron sheets
Scream at us?
Why are our hummocks not our homes?
These walls, being renovated with our blood,
Are they mounted for slogans?
Illegitimate children
Of this habitat
Mark celebrations with ammunitions
Look! Our death
Celebrates birthdays
The white color of our widowed-self
Settled in a grave after getting a divorce
Look! Don't measure our *shalwars
Your sixteen-hours of sleep
Putting burden on our shoulders
Do tell! In which city
Is the strike of funerals observed?

* trousers

Ba Failed Love

On the waves of the ocean
Let's write a letter to sleep
Your treasurable time
That my precious life has eaten
Do you remember those trees
That used to tie our laughs
With their wrists instead of their leaves?
Now rain doesn't fascinate
Did the twilights turn absolute dark?
Why do you watch my hands?
Eyes cannot change fortune lines
Tell me if you can buy the third finger of my left hand
(No . . .)
Don't say
I know this very well
In the subject of fortune
You always get a zero,
And, the subject of Love; I never passed
Let's talk about something else

Sidra Sahar Imran

On Breaths, a 50% Tax Is Not Legitimate

Those who were killed by wars,
Are not going to take
Mathematics exams
Ask me about
The mistaken meanings
Of life's geography
Though death looks
More awful than that of hate
History
Is being written with red ink
Trenches are crying
Someone has mistaken the course
Someone eats his breaths
After dipping it into life's grave
But those who are addicted to explosives
Can't curtail themselves
From writing love letters of ammunition
Who will tell it to the addicted culprits
That there is no photostat to life?

A Vacant Space for Angels

I

When five bodies
Lay in your homes
Then illiterate mothers
Start taking full numbers
In mathematics
Zero comes before one
But that carries no value for you

II

White coffins on colored beds
Crush their beauty
Eyes on a snowy day
Are frozen in our bodies
Bring some fire to run tears down the eyes

III

To win;
When you all
Bark at each other
Frozen bodies beg
O, dogs!
Go somewhere else
And lick stones!

Sidra Sahar Imran

The Barren Side of the Sun

We haven't tasted the sunlight
What does that light resemble?
What are these birds?
We pen trees as lamps,
Oxygen as death,
And leaves are our tears
We are not aware
Why the color of heaven
Is blue like our emotions
We are not acquainted with the flight of steps
We sleep enfolding our eyes with walls
We ascertain coffins
Of our flowers in funeral yards,
And distinguish rains with our eyes
On the nights when they are short of salt
On lifeless woods
We decorate our days
Look! Our dreams grew dry
Now, for us,
Build houses without windows

A Poem Written on a Death Certificate

This man's language
Wants to cut
Who for the first time
Established the tradition of foot licking

In the hands of this girl
I want to write
Who for the first time
Touched a man's feet

I want to stone this mother
Who tore his daughter's dreams
Cover your son's books
And give the daughter a stinking husband
The smell of the room coming from the son
Ignored

To this father
In a burning pile of rubbish
Who wants to suppress
In whose bed
A virgin girl became pregnant
And the daughter,
Driven out from the place of honor

Sidra Sahar Imran

Death Rehearsals
in the Days of a Pandemic

Wearing isolation shoes
We're living in second-hand graves
After placing us in isolation machines
We're being taught the lessons
If you're fighting a war with death
Don't run away
After being hit by a bullet on our back
Our chests are waving like flags
Death is showering with full intensity
In all cities
Even when it is not a rainy season
Or monsoon

Suffocating in our live graves,
We're thinking
In the living mathematics of life
Why we only practice the exercises of minus
The entire day, our eyes are busy
Painting images of funerals on the walls
Even if we won't take
Anyone's eyes with us
Neither a smile
Nor farewell kisses
"Alas! Does someone die a curfew death?"
This question has not been asked
Before today

We, just by living with our own eyes
Engage ourselves in self-conversation
That, when this connection is disconnected,
We'll be shifted to plastic bags
From our second-hand graves

D for Death

Take off your shoes
And feel . . .
The intense pain of what went missing

Construct a room without any windows
And feel . . .
Would you love the grave?

Call your name loudly into the ears of the city
If no one comes, then it's for you to understand
That you've got the reward of two yards of land

Celebrate – if
Starving children in village mosques
Got stuck on lessons
Of Manna and the *Quails!

* Heavenly food mentioned in the Bible and the Quran

Sidra Sahar Imran

An Expensive War and a Cheap Woman

If your heart gets full
Put on your shoes
In the holes of my wrap
I am living like a nail
Under the soles of your feet
Your pain fears of . . .
I make birds of freedom
Your fists have the keys to my hair
Languages like your abstinence
If opened
The border will turn into a nude painting
Dance
On the stage of my shirt
Stare
At the bones of my body
Fill your cheeks with applauses
We have guns with guns
In your laughter
My eyes went back
If anyone had a blizzard
And went to a river
The water will tear your kidneys
The wells will turn upside down
Before I had time to come
To correct the geography of your body
Otherwise
A woman from the fire of your impotence
The foundation of the new hell

The March of Homeless Women

I am at a distance of a knocking kick
From my door and from the reach of wolves
They tear my blouse
With the nails of their shoes
I attack them like an injurious bird
My nails cannot pull out their dirty eyes
They hit my rip cage with their laugh
Bark at me
Ask me . . . "where are the bastards?"
I pull out their tongues
The trigger of rifles
(The pain of a bad word is stronger than
the pain of a bullet)

Sidra Sahar Imran

Poems for Palestine, I

I

Life is crawling
On a wheelchair
And tears got deaf
By listening to intense
Explosions
To whom I ask
To showers
Few laughs
On my father's grave
(Today is his birthday)

II

We've gathered
Color pencils
And butterflies,
And an army gathered
Small-sized graves
(Alas! We'd collected flowers)

III

An army
Was digging
Walls of our houses
I turned myself
Into small stones
My sister
Had nothing but me

IV

There are
Only two eyes
To mourn
Over six coffins
Tell me,
O Creator of eyes,
Who will compensate
My remaining salt?

Poems for Palestine, II

I

What does a smile mean?
We don't know
We opened our eyes
To the noise of explosions
We haven't smelled
The fragrance of roses
We are doing the business
Of smelling coffins
From childhood on
We walk wearing death
In our feet
And life like pebbles
In our hands
Alas!
With the support
Of these pebbles
We could distribute
Death Identity cards
To all occupied armies in the world

II

There is a book
In my bag
In this book
There is no word
Such as
B for Bomb
Then . . .

Who provided you
With those books
Which taught you
K for Kill?

III

Uncle,
You have killed
My parents
They used to
Love your kids
As much
As they used to love me
Then you asked
My siblings
To run very fast
And opened fire on them
With a loud laugh
Tha . . . Tha . . . Tha
You have one bullet
Loaded in your gun
You can shoot me too
(A Palestinian kid to an Israeli Army soldier)

IV

I sent a dove
To God
After making it
From mud
That dove
Will bring
Olive branches

Sidra Sahar Imran

From God
Then
I'll cultivate
Those olives
On my land
And
Will request
The Almighty
To forbid
Red color
On this land

Death's Rehearsals

Epilogue

About the Author

Poet, novelist, fiction writer, essayist, and playwright Sidra Sahar Imran hails from Karachi, Pakistan. She was born on August 8, 1986 to a very traditional family. She received her early education in Karachi. She earned her Master's degree in Urdu literature from the University of Karachi. Already as a child, she fell in love with words and books, and that love transformed her to one of most of powerful and rebellious voices of contemporary Urdu Literature.

Sidra Sahar Imran started writing creatively in early childhood. Later on, she wrote poetry, novels, fictional work, articles and columns. Her work in Urdu has been published in numerous journals and magazines of Pakistan and India. She also wrote novels for business publications. Her two poetry books, *Moot Ki Rehearsal* (*Death's Rehearsals*) and *Hum Gunah ka Istahara Hein* (*We: The Metaphors of Sin*) have been received most favorably by critics and readers. As a playwright, she is associated with different TV channels in Pakistan.

About the Translator

Poet, translator and writer Muhammad Azram hails from Haripur, Pakistan. He is an autodidact and a self-styled philosopher. In his literary work, Azram opens himself to a multitude of subjects that vary from traditional themes of love and relationships to the time, space and life-trio, and to more challenging focal points like life and death and beyond the known and unknown. While he pens down his own intellectual interests, he also translates powerful voices from the Urdu literature.

Muhammad Azram has been recognized with numerous awards and honors by various international literary organizations. His contributions to anthologies of global acclaim and solo books continue to be published worldwide. A selection of his work has been translated into many languages, including Spanish, French, Italian, Serbian, and Arabic, and have appeared in prestigious publications.

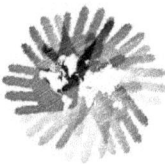

www.ingramcontent.com/pod-product-compliance
Lightning Source LLC
Chambersburg PA
CBHW060127050426

42448CB00010B/2030